Sexual Difficulties in Marriage

DAVID MACE

Fortress Press   Philadelphia

Library of Congress Catalog Card Number 72–75652
ISBN 0–8006–1108–X

3234A72   Printed in the United States of America   1–1108

Series

Introduction

Pocket Counsel Books are intended to help people with problems in a specific way. Problems may arise in connection with family life, marriage, grief, alcoholism, drugs or death. In addressing themselves to these and similar problems, the authors have made every effort to speak in language free from technical vocabulary.

Because these books are not only nontechnical but also brief, they offer a good start in helping people with specific problems. Face-to-face conversation between counselor and counselee is a necessary part of the help the authors envision through these books. The books are not a substitute for person-to-person counseling: they supplement counseling.

As the reader gets into a book dealing with his concerns, he will discover that the author aims at opening up areas of inquiry for further reflection. Thus through what is being read that which needs to be said and spoken out loud may come to the surface in dialog with the counselor. In "working through" a given problem in this personal way, help may come.

WILLIAM E. HULME
General Editor

To Bill and Gini Masters

courageous pioneers

brilliant researchers

skillful counselors

cherished friends

with my admiration and gratitude

Contents

Introduction:

What This Book
Offers You

If you are having sex difficulties in your marriage, at least you are in good company. The Masters[1] have expressed the opinion that about half of all married couples develop sexual problems of one kind or another. This may make you feel a little better. But it does not solve your problem, and that is your real need. I am writing this book in the hope that I can help you. As far as it is possible to counsel through the pages of a book, I am offering to be your counselor.

This means that you should know something about my qualifications. I can best describe myself as a behavioral scientist. I am currently a professor in a medical school, where my main task is to encourage and train medical students to do a good job in dealing with the sexual and marital problems of their patients. During most of my life I have been busy promoting marriage counseling all over the world. For seven years I was Executive Director of the American Association of Marriage and Family Counselors. Over a period of nearly forty years I have counseled with many people who sought help in meeting all kinds of marital problems. During these years I have taken the sex histories of well over a thousand men and women.

1. Dr. William Masters and Mrs. Virginia Johnson. They have been known as "Masters and Johnson." But they are now married, and I suppose they should be called the Masterses. That sounds very awkward, so I have decided to call them the Masters.

Making use of these experiences, and of opportunities to learn from other therapists, I have tried to equip myself to help people in trouble. I am far from satisfied with either my knowledge or my skill, because this is a complex field. But at least I feel I have come a long way since I started, and have gained a far better understanding of marital-sexual difficulties. I find I can now move with confidence in dealing with problems that would have made me feel pretty insecure in my early days as a sex counselor. For this reason I offer you encouragement and hope. Because of our much better understanding of sexual difficulties today, the chances of overcoming them are much better than they have ever been before.

Now I have introduced myself. But what about you? Unfortunately you can't respond by telling me about yourself personally. Yet I believe that the most helpful way to write this book will be for me to talk to you directly, as though you were sitting with me in the same room. I don't know what your special problem is, but since I plan to go over all the problems of sexual inadequacy we know about I am pretty sure to touch on yours. And it so happens that the underlying causes of most marital-sexual difficulties are very much the same, so I think that when I discuss the basic reasons why these problems arise, and the basic ways of clearing them up, I shall be talking to you pretty directly most of the time.

Since the purpose of this book is to offer you practical help, let me tell you now at the beginning how I shall try to do this. Effective help may involve you in three steps.

First you will need to have certain basic *information*, and I shall try to supply it. The solving of problems requires some understanding of why these problems occurred in the first place. When your car stalls on a lonely road, you have to wait until an auto mechanic arrives. You are yourself physically capable of doing everything he might do, but your trouble is that, not understanding how the car functions, you have no means of deciding what is the right thing to do. In fact, then, you can't fix your car because you lack essential knowledge. Likewise, many husbands and wives can make no progress in overcoming their sexual difficulties because they don't understand just why these difficulties have arisen. I shall try, even in this short book, to explain to you in essence what lies behind marital-sexual problems, because such knowledge is an essential ingredient in the treatment. Some of this knowledge has come to us quite recently as a result of new research; you may not find it in older books about sex.

The second thing that will be necessary will be a willingness on your part—here I am talking to you both, husband and wife together —to *experiment with new approaches*. No sex problem was ever solved merely by reading a book, by listening to a lecture, or even by taking a course. I suspect that, if you are really bothered by your problem, you have already read everything you could lay your hands on that seemed to touch on it in any way; and maybe you have also asked a few people for advice. But if that is all you have done, it is simply not enough. Sex problems can't be solved *in your head*. They can be solved only by applying your new understanding to your total way of living together as husband and wife and relating to each other in mind and spirit as well as in body. I shall have more to say about this later, but I want to emphasize right now that it is absolutely essential for success. A marital-sexual problem is not the problem of one person. It is the joint problem of two persons, and can only be solved by changes in their relationship brought about by improved communication and cooperation.

A third possible need will be *the help of a qualified personal counselor*. I say "possible" because you *might* be able to clear up your problem by yourselves, simply through experimenting along the lines I will suggest to you. I will certainly try to be a counselor to you and I may succeed. But it is quite difficult to counsel effectively on a one-sided basis, when no face-to-face encounter with the counselee is possible. So even if you cooperate fully with me and with one another, the reading and experimentation may not prove to be enough. In that event, I shall urge you to seek direct professional counseling, and tell you how to go about it. If this turns out to be necessary, though, the efforts you have already made, based on the reading of this book, will not be wasted. You will go to a counselor much better prepared, as a result of these efforts, to work effectively with him.

Indeed, it is quite possible that your counselor may have given you this book, asking you to read it as a part of your cooperation with him. The book contains a good deal of general information that all married couples should have when they seek counseling help. Moreover, it can save the counselor's time and free him to concentrate on the personal, dynamic aspects of your particular problem, if he can assume in advance that you have this general knowledge. You will also understand better what he is trying to do for you, and thus be enabled to cooperate with him more effectively.

These, then, are the clear conditions I must make for the solution of your problem. Study this book till you understand clearly what it tells you. Talk together freely as husband and wife about what you learn, and try out in practice what is suggested to you. If after doing all this to the best of your ability the problem is still with you, take it to a qualified professional counselor for more intensive aid.

If you will faithfully carry out these instructions, your chances of success should be quite good. We have knowledge about these difficulties today that we did not have before. We have better qualified sex counselors, and more of them, than we ever had before. These resources are available to you.

1.

The Roles of Sex
in Marriage

This happens to be the nineteenth book I have written. My first book was also a small one, and about sex. Just after it was published my younger daughter, then seven, was asked by a neighbor what the book was about. She replied "I don't exactly know. I haven't read it. But it's called *Does Sex Mortally Matter?*" The real title of the book was *Does Sex Morality Matter?*; yet I have often thought that the other title would have made an equally interesting book!

Does sex mortally matter? To married people, I mean? What exactly *is* it about sex that matters? Is it really necessary at all for a successful marriage? If so, just what needs does it meet, and how?

These may seem to be absurd questions. But they are not. They represent the right point at which to begin. Because, whatever your particular sex problem is, I'm sure you are seeing it as a problem because sex is not doing for you what you believe and expect it should. But where did you get your beliefs and expectations? And are you sure they are reasonable and right?

One of the most important discoveries we have made in recent years is that sexual difficulties seldom have much to do with the state of the physical organs, or even with the way you go about using those organs. Sexual problems have much more to do with your attitudes, your feelings about what ought to happen, or about what ought not to happen.

In the past, people with sexual difficulties generally thought the appropriate step to take was to go to a physician and find out if their sex organs were normal. Or they would read books about how sexual intercourse should be performed—books that put great emphasis on the correct mechanical operations—and try to figure out whether they were pushing the right buttons in the right way at the right moment. If they weren't performing as the book said they should, which usually meant having mutual and simultaneous orgasms, they came to the conclusion that they were doing something wrong. The emphasis was almost entirely on organs of the correct size and shape, and performance that carried out the correct steps in the correct order with the correct timing.

We now know, not only that this whole approach was the wrong one, but that it has actually been the cause of most people's problems. As soon as we begin to think of sexual intercourse as a performance that must be carried out correctly, we brace ourselves, consciously or unconsciously, for the effort. And in so doing, we begin to develop anxiety as to whether we can achieve our goal. The anxiety associated with sexual performance, we now know, is the basic cause of nearly all sexual failures and inadequacies. We shall come back to this later; but I want to affirm right now, before we go any further, that this is the most important thing I have to say to you in this book—and if you don't grasp it clearly before you finish reading, then the book, as far as you are concerned, will have been written in vain.

What Sex Does for Marriage

So I want now to ask you the question: What are you *expecting* sex to do for you, and for your marriage?

There is an idea, widely accepted in American culture, that unless married people have regular sexual intercourse, their marriage is bound to be a disastrous failure. This is not necessarily so. Recent studies have shown that there are marriages in which the couple have never had sexual intercourse at all, and marriages in which they have given up having sexual intercourse years ago; and yet these marriages are holding up, and some of them even seem to be quite happy and successful. I don't want to stress this unduly, because these marriages are not typical and there are probably only a few of them. But just to get the subject into proper perspective, I want to put this fact on record. I have personally, as a marriage counselor, encountered sexless marriages that were very happy marriages. And I have encountered marriages that were so miserable that they broke up, in spite of the fact that the couples concerned had a sexual relationship which the marriage manuals would have viewed as almost a model of perfection.

Sexual performance is therefore not the central factor which decides whether a marriage is happy or unhappy. However, for most couples it is pretty important, and we must ask ourselves why this should be so.

There are in fact three ends which sex serves in marriage: it makes procreation possible; it brings about the satisfaction of certain individual needs of husband and wife; and it provides mutual enjoyment that we now recognize to be a very important form of recreation. I know of no other basic purposes than these three—procreation, individual satisfaction, and shared recreation.

Our Culture's New Understanding of Sex

Our attitudes to these three ends of sex have greatly changed in recent years. In our Western culture, procreation has always, until now, come first, satisfaction next, and recreation has scarcely been recognized at all. Today there is a tendency almost to reverse the order, which is what the "sexual revolution" is all about.

The chief aim of marriage in the past has been to have children— to continue the family line and to keep up the population. These goals determined the prevailing attitudes toward marriage. A childless union was often regarded as a disaster, whether the couple were otherwise happy together or not. On the other hand, the view was taken that sexual intercourse in marriage is so closely linked to procreation that for centuries, at least until the time of the Reformation and even beyond, the Christian church taught that where the intention of having children is not present devout married couples should not practice sexual intercourse. Instead they were expected to abstain from all sexual activities as a healthy exercise in self-control, and as a token that they were truly spiritually-minded.

Nowadays how do we view all this? Our concern about population has gone into reverse. We are now told that overpopulation of the earth is the greatest single menace to our human future, and that responsible married couples should on no account have more than two children. For a fertile couple, this could in theory be accomplished by two acts of sexual intercourse in a lifetime. More realistically, it would probably be accomplished by having intercourse occasionally during only two separate periods, of several weeks or months duration, during an entire lifetime. In the total span of married life today, however, sexual intercourse undertaken for the express purpose of procreation has shrunk to an activity of minor importance.

If of course your sexual problem is that you are unable to achieve conception at all, I recognize it to be a serious one for you. Parenthood is one of life's great and rewarding experiences, and no one has the right to deny any couple the two children that represent the desirable family size. If, however, you are able to have normal intercourse but not to achieve pregnancy, this book will not help you much with your problem. What you must do is to go together to a physician who specializes in the treatment of subfertility. Fortunately, there is a good deal that can be done nowadays to assist you.

As the narrow and exclusive emphasis on sex-for-procreation-only has been challenged, sex in marriage has come to be accepted as a means of meeting all kinds of needs in the marriage partners. The emphasis has been on sex as an expression of their love; and it certainly can and should be just that for any happy, loving couple. However, marriage is a very complex relationship, which goes through all kinds of processes of change and development; and the old-fashioned starry-eyed concept of living happily ever after in a warm steam bath of mutual affection simply doesn't accord with the known facts, even for well-adjusted couples. At least some of the widespread disillusionment about marriage today derives from the fact that the concept of marriage as an automatic source of unending bliss has been culpably and disastrously oversold.

So let's be more realistic, and look at sex in marriage as a means by which a couple can meet each other's needs. This has in fact always been recognized as one of the proper ends of marriage, but in a one-sided way. The sexual needs of men were given a good deal of attention, while those of women were hardly recognized at all. Wives were told that it was their duty to accord to their husbands their "marriage rights," which meant that wives must be available for intercourse at any reasonable time that their husbands desired it. The church tolerated this arrangement by saying that sexual intercourse in marriage, as well as being the means of procreation, could be permitted as "a remedy against sin," meaning that men were by nature wayward creatures and that husbands were less likely to stray from the path of virtue outside marriage if their wives nobly saw to it that they were kept well satisfied within the marriage bond.

Sexual Needs of Husband and Wife

This view of the woman's duty to meet her husband's sexual needs, regardless of her own feelings, was widely held, even up to the early years of this century. A typical instance was that of an English bride who was advised by her mother, when her husband approached her sexually, to lie quite still and think of the hard-won glories of the British Empire!

As long as women could be persuaded that their destiny was to serve men's needs, this simplified the sex life of the married couple. Sexual intercourse was often not pleasant for those wives; but they accepted it dutifully as the price they paid for the security of being married and economically provided for, and for the fulfillment of their womanhood in having children. By the accepted standards of those times, that was a fair bargain.

However, women are no longer willing to tolerate this subordinate role; and increasingly, men are not willing either to demand that they do so. With the coming of the concept of equality of the partners in marriage, the sexual side of the relationship was soon deep in trouble.

To begin with, the myth that women do not enjoy sex and do not respond vigorously in intercourse, could no longer be maintained. Happily married couples must always have known about female orgasm; but Victorian society somehow managed to suppress the facts, generally by darkly hinting that women who enjoy sex are immoral and bad, so nice women had to learn to conceal their sex feelings and to play in intercourse the passive role assigned to them. With the emancipation of women in other areas, however, the secret was soon out in the open. News of the female orgasm spread rapidly. It was especially welcome among men, because any normal man would prefer a responsive sexual partner to an unresponsive one. But at the same time, it landed many people in trouble. For as soon as the word had been passed round that women could enjoy orgasms just as men did, it was discovered that in fact a number of women could not do so. At first their husbands tended to criticize them for this shortcoming, judging them to be abnormal or deficient. But then the word went round that women don't achieve orgasm at the drop of a hat, but only when they are fully aroused by the polished technique of the well-informed husband. So now the accusing finger swung from the nonorgasmic wives to their supposedly technically inept husbands. The total result of all this was that emancipation brought in its train a great deal of worry and anxiety for both wives and husbands. It was in this setting that the concept of proper sexual performance, and the anxieties that built up around it, began to dominate the sexual scene in our culture.

My suspicion is that your sexual problem, whatever it may be, is somehow linked with this cultural situation; and it is for this reason that I have taken the time to sketch briefly its historical development. Many wives today are having sexual difficulties because, although *intellectually* they are emancipated enough to reject the idea that a woman can be satisfied to lie still while her husband satisfies his sexual needs, *emotionally* they can't free themselves enough to "let themselves go" and achieve full and satisfying orgasm. And many husbands who could have found sexual intercourse satisfactory with the nonresponding woman of the past, now that the situation is complicated by the obligation on their part to satisfy their wives as well as themselves, find the prospect of attempting intercourse, with all the new obligations it now involves, less and less alluring, until finally their own capacity for functioning becomes deranged by the anxiety they generate.

So far I have spoken about the satisfaction of needs in sexual intercourse in very simple terms. I have equated this need with the direct biological drive of sexual desire, a constantly recurring urge in all normal, healthy men and women. However, people feel the need of sex for many reasons other than just plain biological drive. For example, most human cultures put pressure on men to prove their manhood by having sexual intercourse with a woman; and in like manner today's woman may consider herself a failure, in her husband's eyes at least, if she can't produce the orgasms that are now equated with acceptable female sex behavior. So our pride in our gender—meeting the cultural standards of manhood and womanhood—is tied in closely with the quality of our sexual performance.

All sorts of other needs, not directly sexual, also come into the picture. The old idea that a woman must give her husband full sexual satisfaction to keep him at home still survives; indeed, today the fear that he will find somebody else more satisfying is more menacing than ever, because the competition can be pretty keen, and this demands that the wife be a good performer if she is to meet it successfully. And today the husband also has to face the fact that if he doesn't perform well sexually, his wife may soon be looking for a more effective lover elsewhere. Good performance in bed is no longer simply a way of making the marriage run more smoothly; nowadays it may literally be the only way of holding the marriage together at all. This is especially true in a time when many men and women have sexual experiences before marriage, with several partners. If the sexual performance of the marriage partner doesn't measure up to that of a highly skillful previous lover, he or she is going to be rated a failure; and this judgment will sooner or later communicate itself, consciously or unconsciously, and often with paralyzing effect.

Sexual performance, therefore, is tending to become one of the standards by which a person rates his worth; and if performance is poor, this may have devastating consequences for his self-esteem. So sex, far beyond the meeting of our biological needs, is becoming one of the most important ways in which we meet our needs for social acceptance and approval.

At this point it may be helpful to you to ask yourself, frankly and realistically, the question I asked at the beginning of this chapter: What exactly is it about sex that matters to you? The question can be divided conveniently into two: (1) What exactly do I expect sex to do for me? (2) Why exactly am I so upset because sex seems not to be working right in my marriage? If you could sit down and write out all the reasons you can think of, sexual and nonsexual, you might make some interesting discoveries about yourself that will be helpful to us later on.

Sex as Recreation

Now let's consider the third purpose of sex—recreation. Notice that the meaning of this word is re-creation, or renewal. Only in recent years have we been willing to recognize that sex is a form of play—a delightful, carefree experience of mutual enjoyment, which brings light and gaiety to brighten the often dull routines, not to mention the burdensome responsibilities, that are an inevitable part of family life.

Our Puritan background has frowned on this idea of sex as fun. H. L. Mencken once defined the Puritan as a person who suffers from an overwhelming dread that somewhere, sometime, somehow, someone may be enjoying himself. This is a rather extreme judgment; but it is certainly true that our religious forebears took a very serious view of life, and regarded both sex and fun with profound suspicion; so naturally enough, the idea of having fun with sex was

8

under a double judgment, and we tend to be very uncomfortable about any such idea.

In other cultures, sex as pure enjoyment has been accepted more realistically. Among some of the South Pacific islanders, the enjoyment of sex is openly accepted. Among Indian peasants, whose life of grinding poverty and ceaseless toil offers so few satisfactions of other kinds, sex is esteemed as the great event in which sorrow may for a time be forgotten, and the spirit released in an experience of soaring ecstasy.

In our own culture this side of sex is now gradually being given more attention. The marriage manuals use terms like "foreplay" and "love play" to describe the preliminaries to sexual intercourse, and speak of the period following the climax as the "after-glow." Yet many of us still cannot feel comfortable about playful bodily caresses, and about all the teasing advances and retreats of the erotic play that precedes intercourse, so dramatically demonstrated in the elaborate courtship rituals of some birds and in the erotic dances of primitive peoples. A pervasive guilt paralyzes the capacity of many husbands and wives to play sexual games with one another. Their rigid sense of propriety even confines them to one correct way of having intercourse—the so-called missionary position—and shrinks from all experimentation and variety as it shrinks from sin.

Add all this up, and it is easy to see why so many people are having trouble with sex. What should be play has become work. An experience that should be embarked upon with carefree abandonment is approached instead with anxious concern lest we fail to do it right. Instead of forgetting ourselves in a gay whirl of delirious joy, we watch ourselves anxiously to make sure that every step is correctly made and correctly timed. The result is that stress and strain have invaded one of life's fundamental recreational activities, and we end up unable to perform because we are unable to relax and allow our bodies to take over and function with the ancient wisdom that is far broader and deeper than the contrived, cultivated wisdom of our minds. How this creates problems for us will become clear as we continue.

2.

The Complexity of
Sexual Intercourse

A physician friend of mine, looking at a porcupine, once remarked to me, "Isn't it amazing that creatures made like that ever manage to reproduce?" The porcupine isn't the only one either. Among the vast variety of creatures, great and small, that inhabit our planet, there are many others for whom the task of coming together sexually is full of complications. Yet they all manage to do it—otherwise they would not survive.

Physical and Emotional Involvement

For human beings, sexual intercourse is relatively easy. At least this is so from a *physical* point of view. The penis of the human male can normally find its way into the female vagina without difficulty, either from the front or from behind. However, physical barriers do occasionally occur. A man may have a penis that isn't the right shape (the size doesn't matter), or the foreskin may be tight and uncomfortable. A woman may have a hymen so tough that it needs to be opened up by simple surgery, or she may even have to be provided with an artificial vagina (this can be done). But these are rare conditions. If you suspect anything of this kind in yourself or your partner, don't hesitate to go and get medical advice about it. The man should go to a urologist, the woman to a gynecologist.

In terms of our physical makeup, therefore, we humans should hardly ever have sexual difficulties. But we do, and the explanation lies in the fact that we very easily develop *emotional* troubles about sex. The Masters, whose researches in this field have been of outstanding importance, explain that our sexual desires are controlled by two different influences: the biophysical, related to our bodies; and the psychosocial, related to our minds. Nearly all human sexual difficulties are psychosocial in origin. That is why I started this book by talking about our *attitudes* to sex, and not about our physical sex organs. I am simply going to assume that you know the elementary facts about the structure and function of your sex organs, and will not waste any of my limited space on anatomy and physiology.

What I want to do in this chapter is to provide a brief description of what happens when two people have sexual intercourse, from the point of view of their feelings and responses. This will give me an opportunity to point out the various difficulties that can arise, both for the man and the woman. Then, later on, I will return to these difficulties, and describe the forms of treatment that have been found most effective in clearing them up.

If husband and wife are to have sexual intercourse in a manner that is satisfying to them both, four requirements would normally be met: each would have normal and healthy sex organs (in the overwhelming majority of cases this can be taken for granted); each would have a normal heterosexual drive (the desire to unite sexually with an attractive person of the opposite sex); each would be sexually stimulated and attracted by the other (this is often referred to as being "in love," though the word "love" has a much wider meaning); and each would be free from negative emotional feelings like fear, anxiety, guilt, shame, revulsion, or resentment, so that they would approach intercourse with happy, comfortable feelings about it. If in any given instance any of these four ingredients should be missing, either in the husband or in the wife, the particular experience of intercourse might turn out to be frustrating or unsuccessful for one partner or for both. This means that there are eight possible points at which intercourse could turn sour or go wrong. So it could almost be said that, emotionally, human beings are somewhat like porcupines as far as sex is concerned. And it may be added that the more sensitive and "civilized" people are, the more they are likely to have difficulties—because of their higher expectations.

Not only must four conditions be met for successful sexual intercourse; there are also four areas in which married people must achieve sexual adjustment. They must manage successfully each individual act of intercourse, so that it is satisfying to both. They must agree about how frequently, and when and where, they will come together sexually. They must keep a proper balance between their sex desires and their personal relationship with one another. And they must control procreation, by some means of contraception, in a way that is acceptable to both. Complications can arise in any or all of these areas.

Management of the Sex Act

The management of the act of sexual intercourse requires a certain amount of skill. Who makes the first move? Traditionally the husband did, but nowadays there is nothing improper about the wife asking for intercourse if she desires it. *How* is the request for intercourse made? Some couples will make it in words. Some who can never bring themselves to use words will develop signals to indicate their wishes. The double bed greatly facilitates this nonverbal process—an exploring hand reaching out to make contact, or an affectionate embrace, can be the understood signal. But what if one makes the approach, and the other just doesn't feel responsive? The wife may be starting a period; the husband may be too tired; either one may not be feeling well, or may be irritated with the other for some reason. How does the one who made the advance accept a rebuff? We are very sensitive about sexual desires, and sometimes when we find ourselves turned down our pride is so deeply hurt that we find it hard to make another advance at a later time. There are gracious ways of making a negative response, but we are not always gracious. Is it sometimes best to try to respond positively, even if you don't feel like it? Maybe your mood will change when you get started, and you will eventually enjoy it. But what if your mood *doesn't* change? Do you *pretend* you're enjoying it, even if you aren't, in order to avoid disappointing your partner? Or would that be dishonest? Is it best just to admit that you aren't turned on, but that you are nonetheless willing to try. But then what should your partner do? Accept your willingness to try, and go ahead, hoping for the best? Or give up and look for better luck next time? And if after you do give up, your sex desire continues to bother you so that you can't sleep, how do you avoid feeling angry and resentful?

These are all quite common, everyday situations in married life. You can see what tangles couples can get into if they are unable to deal with these situations comfortably. And you can imagine the predicament of couples who can't *talk* with each other about their sexual feelings and needs, and yet have to handle situations of this kind. Good, open communication about sexual responses, based on a healthy and natural acceptance of sexual needs as being entirely right and good in marriage, is obviously essential. How do you manage all this? Is it possible that part of your trouble lies here? Whether you think so or not, I would like you both to take a good look at this area before you go any further. How good is your sexual communication? Are there points at which you need to improve it?

Once the advance is made (by either partner) and responded to by the other, what next? The instructions given in the early marriage manuals, amounting to a series of mechanical operations, should be avoided like the plague. No two couples will necessarily act alike, and no one couple will necessarily act alike on two different occasions. However, there are certain stages in the development of sexual intercourse which most of us go through, so we ought to know what they are. We used to recognize three of these stages, but the Masters's research has extended them to four: excitement, plateau, orgasm, and resolution. They simply record the natural sequence of events—the rising of sexual desire to a peak, the explosive release in the orgasm, and the dying away of desire and return to a normal emotional state.

The excitement phase usually begins in one partner, and when he communicates the fact that he is sexually aroused, this starts up a response state of arousal in the other. What they do next is for them to decide, and will depend on what each knows is pleasing to the other—speaking words of love, kissing, caressing each other's bodies. Whatever will intensify sexual desire in both of them is appropriate. There should be no rules and no limitations about the sex play of lovers, as long as both desire and both enjoy what is done. Van de Velde, whose marriage manual has been a classic for more than a generation, simply says, "Whatever is physiologically sound is also ethically right." In other words, do whatever comes naturally, as long as you break no bones!

Here again, communication is essential. How can a couple know what is sexually exciting to each other, except by trying a multitude of experiments and reporting what feels good and what doesn't? The books give you some good general hints about what to try, but love play must be individual, not general. The standard story here is about the wife who said, "I hate that book. I know just when my husband gets to the bottom of page 8 and starts on page 9. It's always the same. It makes me want to scream. He treats me like a machine, not a woman."

The aim at this stage, of course, is to raise excitement to the highest possible pitch. But sometimes things go wrong. The husband inadvertently hurts his wife, and she snaps at him angrily, as if he had done it on purpose. His feelings are hurt and his sexual desire rapidly dies away. Or she hears a disturbing sound and begins to worry about whether the children may come rushing into the bedroom. Then her desire collapses like a punctured balloon. Many accidental events may stop the surge of sexual arousal, and sometimes it is quite difficult to get started again.

There are more serious difficulties that can arise at this point. Distress feelings exactly like those I have just described can also be stirred up, in husband or wife, *from within*. Nothing outside blocks the husband or brings him discouragement, yet his desire dies away as a wave of panic rushes through him. No external disturbance prevents the wife from responding to her husband's caresses, yet free-floating anxiety begins to surge within her until the idea of sexual intercourse becomes unwelcome and even repulsive.

Fear and the Paralysis of Sexual Response

What has happened? Fear triggered off by the rising sexual excitement rises with it and entwines itself about the sexual urge like ivy choking a young sapling, and as fear mounts it overwhelms sexual desire and brings it down. There is in us all a protective mechanism that will not allow sexual desire to continue when we experience anxiety. In the life of the wild, self-preservation takes priority over all other feelings or wishes. So, in the presence of danger, sex refuses to function. Some animals are so sensitive on this point that they will not breed in captivity. They cannot feel secure enough to allow their sexual urges full expression.

Behind this braking mechanism lies a fear of intercourse—sometimes a deep, irrational fear that is hard to identify and bring to the surface. The fear has always been implanted by some unpleasant, negative association in the past—even way back in childhood. It is as if a small accusing voice deep inside you warned, "Don't do that! It's wrong. It's dangerous. You may get hurt. Don't do it."

The pulling down of sexual desire can manifest itself outwardly. In the man this takes two forms. First, he may lose his erection; his penis becomes soft and flabby, and he can't go on. This is a form of what we call "impotence," a word which just means "no power." The other possibility is that he retains his erection, but reaches the climax and ejaculates very quickly, so that he has no time to go on to intercourse. This is a form of what we call "premature ejaculation"—going off too soon. Both of these experiences are of course very embarrassing to the husband, because his wife is waiting for him to proceed to intercourse, and he leaves her high and dry. He sees himself as a failure in her eyes, and unless she has been very sympathetic and understanding, he will approach her the next time with the shameful memory of his failure added to the underlying fear that is of course still there. The result is that each new failure will help to create the conditions for an even more dismal failure next time.

In the woman no erection has to be maintained, so her reaction is different. She may simply close the door. Her muscles tighten up around the entrance of the vagina, and it shuts like a trap. This muscle spasm is called "vaginismus," and usually it completely prevents the penis from getting in. Even if the wife is willing to let her husband go ahead, her intellectual consent is canceled out by her emotional protest, which is usually beyond the control of her conscious mind. Even if she insists that she is willing, the husband soon gives up trying, and after successive failures further attempts at intercourse may be abandoned.

We shall discuss these difficulties in more detail later. In both men and women, what they are really saying is, "I'm afraid to have intercourse with you, because something tells me I may suffer some terrible harm if I do. So I'm just not going to do it."

Normally, however, excitement rises and no crippling fears get in the way. A point is reached when desire reaches the plateau phase. This is a point at which the urge to go forward to intercourse is so strong that there is no turning back.

By this time the penis will normally be in position in the vagina, and thrusting movements by both partners in unison bring on the climax for both, separately or together. However, it doesn't necessarily turn out that way. A number of complications are possible.

The husband, after insertion of the penis in the vagina, may lose his erection. He may lose it early or late; but if he does, and fails to reach orgasm, this condition falls into the category of impotence. As he loses his erection, of course, it is very probable that, both physically and emotionally, his sexual drive will die down just when his wife is nearing her climax, and the result may be that she is left aroused but frustrated. This condition, very uncomfortable for her, is likely to produce resentment against her husband, a resentment of which he will almost inevitably become aware and which will intensify his embarrassment and sense of failure.

Obstacles to Female Orgasm

The wife may also run into trouble after the penis enters her vagina. Instead of pleasure, she may experience pain or discomfort. We call this condition "dyspareunia" (pronounced diss-par-you-nee-ah, with emphasis on the first syllable). This awkward word simply means "misfit." The condition takes many different forms. The wife may be dry because she isn't producing enough natural lubrication—in that event a tube of KY Jelly, available at any drugstore, can work wonders. Or she may have some tender spot that needs attention, or even some malformation of her internal sex organs. Any wife who experiences discomfort during intercourse should see a gynecologist, who can check out whether there is any physical cause that needs treatment. Often no physical reason can be found, and the wife even has difficulty in describing the pain in any clear or precise way. When this happens, we may suspect that her problem is emotional. She is in the same condition of anxiety as the wife who develops vaginismus, but her protest is not so vigorous that she shuts the door completely. She is saying, "I let you come in, but I'm not really happy about it, and I wish you would take your penis out again." This is of course very disheartening for the husband, who does not wish to gain sexual pleasure at the cost of giving his wife pain. So he is likely to become discouraged; and although the door is open, he is hesitant to go in because deep down he feels unwelcome.

A final difficulty, and probably the most common of all marital-sexual problems, is orgasm inadequacy in the wife. She gets sexually excited, and welcomes her husband's penis in the vagina. She responds to his thrusting and experiences increasing desire. But she can only rise so far and seems quite unable to reach the summit and go "over the top."

Sometimes the problem may be simply that she doesn't get enough stimulation. The fundamental difference between men and women, in their sexual coming together, is that normally the man initiates and the woman responds. He, of course, also responds to some extent, and she is not deprived of all initiative. But a normal man *can* achieve intercourse with almost any woman; whereas a woman, while she can give herself sexually to any man, can't come to orgasm unless he is able to produce in her a sufficient state of response. So she is dependent on the quality of his performance to a far greater extent than he depends on hers. Although some women are very easily brought to sexual climax, and can in fact reach one climax after another to an extent that is impossible for the man, there are many women who just can't reach orgasm at all unless the conditions are exactly right. Any number of circumstances may tip the scales against success: the husband may be clumsy in his lovemaking; he may not take time enough to arouse her; he may suffer from premature ejaculation, and go off too soon; she may be tired or distracted or not feeling well; she may be at a stage in her monthly cycle when her capacity for response is low.

Fortunately most women don't take very seriously an occasional failure to achieve orgasm. Some in fact expect a certain number of failures and are not concerned as long as these are balanced out by sufficient successes. Some are even content to have only an occasional orgasm now and then. A few even say they don't feel the need for orgasms at all. They enjoy intercourse, the sense of closeness it brings, and the obvious pleasure their husbands derive from it, without feeling the need of anything more for themselves. Sometimes these women are quite content until their husbands begin to make a big fuss over their wives' failure to reach orgasm. Then, touched off by the concern of their husbands, feelings of inadequacy begin to assail them.

The wife who is really in trouble is the one who gets aroused sexually to somewhere near the plateau phase; and then, despite all her efforts and those of her husband, can get no further. Sometimes such couples will go on trying for an hour or more, but the desired orgasm continues to elude the distracted wife. The husband, by now exhausted by his efforts, finally has his orgasm and is soon asleep; while for long hours the wife continues in a state of great emotional tension and frustration, until at long last she succumbs to physical and emotional exhaustion and also falls asleep. These experiences can be very distressing for both, and soon produce a great unwillingness to try again. This experience has been the point at which many husbands and wives, discouraged and disillusioned, have begun to drift apart. Other couples settle for some modified arrangement by which the husband's sexual needs can be met without the wife being aroused to the point at which she may suffer frustration.

Following successful intercourse, the climax for both (it is not important that they reach it together, as some of the older books insisted) leads to the resolution phase. After orgasm, the dying down of sexual tension takes place swiftly and pleasantly, with a pervasive feeling of relaxation and contentment. There is no justification at all for the old Latin saying that after sexual intercourse all creatures are sad. On the contrary, if all has gone well, this should be an experience of great happiness.

Other Areas of Sex Adjustment

Now let me turn to the other areas in which married people need to achieve sex adjustment. Deciding on the frequency of sexual intercourse is a matter for the couple alone to settle. There is no "right" or "normal" frequency. I have known couples who were content with intercourse once a month or even less frequently, and couples who needed it daily or more often. Couples who keep records or try to "pace" themselves are on the wrong track, like mothers who insist on feeding their babies only when the clock strikes the appointed hour. Sex in marriage should be spontaneous and unregulated. Nor is there any "right" time, place, or position. Couples must find out for themselves what suits them best.

There is, however, one problem that arises in this area. Supposing one partner desires intercourse much more often than the other does? This quite often happens, and it can create difficulty. Some people even talk of couples who are "mismated" because their sex desires are not of equal strength. This reveals a rigid attitude to sex. In the next chapter I shall discuss alternative ways of meeting sexual needs, other than through intercourse. By this means a loving, understanding couple can deal quite simply with the problem of differing intensities of sexual desire.

The third area of adjustment is the need to keep a good balance between sexual intercourse and the interpersonal relationship in the marriage. This is an area of the greatest importance, and failure to keep a good balance is the cause of many sexual difficulties. Yet my space is so limited that I shall have to deal with it quite briefly.

Sexual intercourse should ideally be always the expression of love and tenderness between husband and wife. But marriage partners go through periods of conflict, and this is perfectly normal. Two people cannot continue to love each other unless they can from time to time express the hostility that inevitably arises in a close relationship. What happens to sex at such times?

Some would say it should be postponed until the couple have "made up" again. However, sex can sometimes provide the best means for this to take place. Recurrent sexual need is like a magnet that often draws a man and a woman back to each other when they are in danger of drifting apart. So the reconciling role of sex cannot be ignored. The renewed warmth of feeling generated by close body contact may be exactly what is needed to create the conditions for mutual apologies, mutual forgiveness, and reconciliation.

But if the conflicts harden, and the couple continue to have sexual intercourse without resolving their differences, sex loses its personal meaning and becomes more and more shallow and brittle until, finally, the general alienation of the couple makes it such an empty farce that they give it up altogether. Sex is a sweetening influence in marriage, and will bear many burdens; but if we fail to keep the interpersonal relationship in reasonably good repair and there is a degeneration of love, trust, and mutual respect, eventually the sex relationship will collapse and become intolerable. As one wife said to me in reporting that she and her husband had given up sexual intercourse some six months earlier, "You see, there was nothing left for it to express."

The final area of adjustment is concerned with contraception. We have much more reliable means of birth control today than couples had to manage with in the past, although the perfect means of controlling conception has not yet arrived. However, pregnancies still occur by "accident," and often in these cases it turns out that the couple had no clear policy, or that the wife was careless and irresponsible, or that the husband had insisted on intercourse at a time when the wife had run out of pills. Such things ought not to happen. An unwanted pregnancy is a very disturbing experience, and may introduce into the sex life of the couple associations and anxieties that undermine confidence and destroy spontaneity.

When we take a good look at the implications of sexual intercourse for human beings, it is hard to evade the fact that there are plenty of things that can go wrong. From one point of view sex may look very simple—the rhythmic movement of a piston in a cylinder, as Robert Latou Dickinson described it. But, as he then went on to add, appearances are deceptive. In fact, it is really no wonder that people get into trouble in the management of this delicate interaction between a man and a woman, which at its best can be the most deeply satisfying of all human experiences. Its achievement calls for intelligence, skill, and patience. The casual mating of animals, and of primitive people, is an act of individual gratification, and does not provide us with helpful models. A truly mutual sexual experience is an artistic achievement, and people of any refinement will not be satisfied with anything less.

3.

The Uses of
Noncoital Sex

Concluding a two-hour counseling session with a couple who had experienced sexual difficulties, I said in the course of my summing up, "I would like you to give up all attempts at sexual intercourse for at least a month."

The husband's jaw dropped. "What?" he exclaimed, "No sex for a whole month?"

"Excuse me," I replied, "I didn't say 'no sex.' I only said 'no sexual intercourse.' There's quite an important difference. In fact, I want you to have plenty of sex—but only of the kind you can handle in the present state of your relationship."

The Masters, in developing their new and highly effective approach to the treatment of sexual inadequacy, have made extensive use of what they call the "sensate focus." Before I heard them speak of this, I had in my own counseling developed the same idea, but I had called it "pre-erotic tactile sensitization." Let me explain what all this means.

In the previous chapter we saw how complicated sexual intercourse can become when it fails to meet expectations. The whole experience, which should be one of delight, becomes instead a nightmare, and is anticipated with increasing anxiety. After a time, attempts at intercourse may be given up altogether. It isn't at all unusual to find a couple in marital conflict who have not come together sexually for months, even for years. I recently asked one unhappy wife in her sixties when she and her husband had last had intercourse; she said, "Fifteen years ago."

22

These people say they have "given up sex"; but I find this is not true. Even if they think they have, sex has certainly not given *them* up. Almost all people who go into marriage have sexual needs, and these needs don't go away when intercourse is discontinued. Most of them masturbate. Some of them experiment with extramarital sex on the side—only to find, quite often, that they still have sex problems. Even those who say they have no direct sex "outlets" of any kind usually admit to having sex dreams and fantasies, and to being plagued by unwelcome sexual desires. The few who say they have no sexual interests of any kind usually turn out to be the most emotionally disturbed of all, because they are suppressing not only sex, but their awareness of their own interest in sex, and as a result living in a world of unreality and make-believe.

Giving up sexual intercourse, therefore, is not giving up sex. Because sexual desire is still there even though it is denied satisfaction, a married couple inevitably tend to blame each other for their states of individual frustration, and to develop a great deal of resentment which they vent on one another openly or indirectly. This leads to petty cruelty and nastiness which can poison their relationship, and the venom sometimes pours out like a flood in the conjoint sessions in which the marriage counselor encourages them to bring their suppressed emotions out into the open.

In one way, all this hatred is a massive defense against the temptation to try intercourse again and register another shattering failure. While two people are living together in a state of mutual hostility, they are not likely to make sexual advances to one another. So, behind the wall of hate, they feel safe—but miserably safe, of course.

I wonder whether you can recognize what I am describing? Perhaps your own sexual difficulties have brought you to this unpleasant situation, in one form or another. It is the situation that confronts the marriage counselor again and again when couples with sexual problems come to him for help. The couple are caught in a trap and seem unable to move in any direction. They have sexual needs, but they can't acknowledge them to one another; or if they do, and try to have intercourse, it doesn't go right and only makes the situation

23

worse. The only path that seems open to them is backward and out of the marriage. But shrinking from such a drastic step, they seek marriage counseling.

In the early years, we marriage counselors handled this situation rather poorly. We thought the problem was to find out why sexual intercourse wasn't working right; we tried to analyze the feelings and reactions of the spouses in great detail, and to trace the origins of their present attitudes in their earlier life experiences. We generally did this with the partners separately, seeking to restore their sexual capacity and confidence so that they could resume intercourse and do better than before. Sometimes we succeeded—but more often we failed.

There were two serious and fundamental errors in this approach. The first was our failure to recognize that the problem was not simply an individual one for either partner, but the result of a deadlocked relationship in which real communication, and the ability to express positive feeling of any kind, had broken down. I now believe that for most couples these deadlocked relationships can be dealt with only by opening up the channels of communication between them. This means first of all getting the negative feelings out and openly expressed between them; only then will the channels be free for positive feeling to begin to flow again.

This is often a difficult task. The couple are usually "frozen" into a state of mutual hostility, and the ice literally has to be broken. Couples sometimes *can* do this by themselves, by sitting down together and honestly opening their minds and hearts to one another. More often, they need a skilled counselor to draw them out and teach them, in conjoint sessions, how to accept each other's anger and resentment without retaliating and setting up what I call the "artillery duel" interaction.

In this difficult task of bringing a couple back to each other and thawing out the cold, hard attitudes they have developed, sex can play an important part. Sex can generate an atmosphere of warmth and generosity and forgiveness, all of which are sorely needed. But if the couple's problem has been caused by, or aggravated by, difficulties in having sexual intercourse, it might be quite disastrous to send them back to that battlefield, on which they have already suffered wounds and defeat.

Freeing Sex from Performance Fears

It is in this critical situation that one can find a happy solution in "noncoital sex." I chose the title of this chapter carefully. I didn't want to call it "sex without intercourse," because "intercourse" means good communication between people, and that's one of the goals we are trying to achieve. So I used the Latin word "coitus," which means a getting together, in this case by putting the penis into the vagina. What I mean by "noncoital sex" is any kind of sex play as long as you don't put the penis in the vagina.

We are now looking at sex, of course, as *recreation*. We have already seen that this is a rather new idea in our culture, and one about which we are not entirely comfortable. But I think we must learn to accept it, because our failure to do so plays a great part in creating, and sustaining, most of our marital-sexual difficulties. And it can be used very effectively in solving those problems, as I now want to explain.

I started this chapter by telling you how I advised a particular couple to give up sexual intercourse altogether for at least a month. Why did I say that?

These two people had a sex problem. They were feeling miserable about their failure. Their misery was focused in their unsuccessful attempts to have intercourse in a way that would measure up to their expectations. Their thinking about sex was therefore focused on intercourse, and their thinking about intercourse was focused on their sense of failure. All this was very negative. They had not yet given up hope and abandoned intercourse, as other couples have done. But I knew this could very well happen in time.

So, by asking them to give up intercourse, I took them off the hook. I relieved them of the fear that they would not be able to perform successfully. This was really a great relief to them both, as they admitted afterwards. The husband protested at the time, but it was really a hollow protest, made to protect his masculine pride. Inside himself he was quite glad. For at least a time I had removed a shadow from their lives.

But I had no intention of putting them into a sexual vacuum. What I wanted to do was to simplify sex for them to a level at which there were no performance fears, no demands. In this way I hoped to remove their anxiety and enable them to discover the fact that sex is really fun. I wanted them to go back to the beginning and start all over again.

When a boy and girl first fall in love, how do they express physically their feelings for one another? They begin by holding hands, rather shyly. Then they kiss. Perhaps he puts his arm around her shoulder, and she responds by snuggling up to him. As their relationship develops, they begin to caress each other more intimately. He may fondle her breasts. Then they touch and caress each other's sex organs. Necking leads to petting, and light petting leads to heavy petting, which usually means petting to climax. How far they go after that depends on their particular ethical code, and we are not concerned about that here. What we *are* concerned about is that they move toward sexual intercourse—whether this happens before or after marriage—by a succession of natural steps that represent gradually increasing intimacy. This has been the accepted pattern for our youth, although that fact has never been widely recognized by their elders. The Puritan idea may be that the couple get no further than a chaste kiss before they go to bed together on their wedding night; but we all know that "it ain't necessarily so." Indeed, it's just as well that it is not so, because such a rapid transition to sexual intercourse could be emotionally very disturbing.

What all this means is that sexual pleasure really rests on a broader base than sexual desire or erotic feeling alone. Body contact, sensory awareness, and communication through touch are vital to us all, as we have been rediscovering lately. All socially organized creatures have to communicate with one another in one way or another; and touch was the means of communication long before language was invented. Touching another person is an act of mutual confidence and mutual acceptance. You don't allow yourself to be touched by someone you know may be hostile to you, because he may treacherously attack you when your guard is down. By the same token, the more intimate the touch, the narrower becomes the circle of those to whom you allow the liberty. You don't kiss everyone with whom you shake hands, and you don't undress in the presence of everyone you kiss. The ultimate intimacies are normally reserved only for a person toward whom you feel entirely positive, and whom you completely trust. With such a person you let your guard down completely; and if it is a loved person of the opposite sex, you are prepared, in whatever circumstances you consider to be appropriate, to share your body completely with the loved one.

Body Contact—Pre-erotic and Erotic

Sexual feeling should therefore rest on this broad base. Of course it is possible to have a sexual encounter with a person with whom you have no broader or deeper relationship at all. But such relationships tend to be very superficial and of short duration. The problem of the Don Juan type of person is that he cannot relate to other people in any depth, so he goes the rounds in a series of "conquests," breaking through the outer defenses of the other person, snatching an experience of intense erotic pleasure, and then running away to avoid the risk of any broader involvement. He is really a very lonely person, and never knows the true meaning of love.

People with sexual difficulties, therefore, almost all need to begin by reestablishing the capacity to enjoy bodily closeness to each other, preferably without sexual arousal at first. Indeed, I have often said that the acid test of a marriage relationship is whether the couple can lie happily and comfortably in each other's arms, without any attempt to arouse each other sexually, and just enjoy being close to each other for its own sake. If they can't do this, they must ask themselves, and each other, *why* they can't. The answer to this question may well provide them with the clue to their real problem. And the problem so revealed, whether sexual or completely nonsexual, is the one on which they must work before they have any real chance to establish, or reestablish, an effectual sexual relationship.

While they work on their interpersonal relationship, they can help the process along by developing their enjoyment of body contact in whatever ways they find to be congenial. The Masters use the word "pleasuring" to describe what the couple do for each other. After undressing, they are encouraged to stroke, rub, and caress each other's bodies in turn. It is not inappropriate to liken this process to the stroking of a pet animal to which you are attached. The "pleasuring" process should not at first include the sex organs. The idea is to build firmly the broader base of enjoyment through non-erotic sensitization, before the more powerful sexual feelings begin to be aroused. But if, of course, sexual responses automatically develop, there is no need to be concerned about this. It is in fact an encouraging sign.

These "pleasuring" sessions should take place in an atmosphere of relaxation and seclusion. In their work at the Reproductive Biology Foundation in Saint Louis the Masters require the couple receiving treatment to leave home and live in a hotel or motel near the counseling center. I have often encouraged a couple, when they were ready for this process of sensitization, to begin by taking a weekend off and going away together to some secluded spot. To begin these exercises in body contact at home may prove very frustrating, because the children may burst into the room, or the telephone may ring, at the most awkward moment. The only way of avoiding this, for many couples, would be to wait until late at night, and by that time they might be too tired to take the procedure seriously or to carry it out with any imagination.

Once the mutual enjoyment of bodily contact has been restored, the couple may move out from this base and begin to experiment with the stirring up of simple erotic responses in each other. All this should be done playfully, with no particular goals in mind. At this point, however, some couples are confronted with a problem. They discover that, despite the fact that they have been married for years, and that they petted freely before that, they are actually embarrassed about handling and stimulating each other's sex organs. Sometimes they will say that this is all "kid stuff." Or they will associate it with masturbation and say they feel it is somehow wrong.

It is therefore necessary to say something about the role of masturbation in marriage. I wish we had another name for it, because the word "masturbation" has gathered to itself all sorts of associations with "secret sin" and "solitary vice" which make many people feel uncomfortable. What I am talking about now is husband and wife bringing each other to the point of orgasm in the marriage bed which is entirely lawful and respectable, but doing it with the penis outside instead of inside the vagina. What is the real difference? The feelings are entirely the same. The Masters's research has shown that all the bodily reactions are identical. So how can one be right and the other wrong?

At this point, whether we like it or not, we are the victims of our cultural past. The ancient Hebrews believed that it was very wicked to "waste" the male semen by depositing it anywhere else than in the female vagina. But this was based on their view that the seminal fluid was in fact the future child, which grew, nourished by the menstrual blood, inside the womb. They knew nothing of the ovum, and nothing of the millions of sperms that are wasted anyway, wherever the semen is deposited. And of course they believed that married couples should have as many children as possible, because increasing the population was a highly meritorious act. We no longer accept these views. Yet the old horror of wasting the semen lives on among us.

The medieval theologians took up the same theme and gave it another twist. They said it was contrary to the natural law to do anything to prevent conception taking place. They also taught that sexual enjoyment of itself was "concupiscence," and therefore sinful. So the idea of a married couple enjoying sex in bed and then not putting the semen where it rightly belonged would have been viewed by them as a very wicked act. These arguments, however, just don't have any meaning nowadays. We perform "unnatural acts" all the time—stomach pumps and eyeglasses and plastic heart valves correct nature's errors and improve on nature's resources. These ancient monks and priests, who were celibate and therefore had renounced sex in all its forms, may have been sincere according to the understanding they had, but we cannot allow their ideas to dominate the lives of married couples in our more enlightened age.

What, then, could possibly be wrong with enjoying sex in marriage to the point of orgasm, without having intercourse? It isn't that I'm arguing *against* intercourse. Couples who can have sex that way, to their complete satisfaction, are welcome to do so. All I'm saying is that, if having sex with intercourse hasn't been satisfying for you, or has become a dreaded experience of repeated failure, it surely would be far better to enjoy noncoital sex than to have no sex at all. I'm not even suggesting this as a permanent arrangement; only as a temporary expedient to tide you over a difficult time, and help you to recover your enjoyment of sex, until you can have a chance to clear up the performance fears that have become associated with intercourse.

A Broader Base for Sexual Response

I therefore recommend to couples who are having sexual difficulties that, after they have established a secure base by recovering their enjoyment of nonerotic body contact, their next step should be to learn to bring each other to orgasm without putting the penis in the vagina. Nearly always, I find that one of the partners is masturbating anyway, and sometimes both are. Usually they have not told each other about this; in which case I encourage them to do so, and the news is often greeted with great surprise. I then suggest that instead of doing it secretly alone, it might be nicer and more pleasant if they did it together, and even helped one another to do it. If, as sometimes happens, the wife has never masturbated, I suggest it would be useful for her to learn, and perhaps for her husband to help her to do so. This suggestion is sometimes greeted with astonishment at first; but when we talk it over together, the couple as a rule soon come to realize that there is really nothing outrageous or unreasonable about it, and from that point they become quite interested.

Practically all married men know how to masturbate, and even those who are completely impotent when they attempt intercourse can usually do so. A husband may find it a little embarrassing at first to use his wife's hand instead of his own; but if she is completely willing to participate, this awkwardness soon passes. When the wife can masturbate by herself, using the hand of a willing and cooperative husband instead of her own is no great problem. Where she has never been able to masturbate, it is probably better that she should learn by herself first, using an electric vibrator if necessary to get started. It is best for one partner not to try to bring the other to climax alone. A great deal has been written about husbands stimulating their wives sexually by manipulation of the clitoris. In fact, the average husband cannot do this, even with instructions from his wife, as well as she can do it if she takes his hand in hers and guides it so as to make just the right movements with just the right amount of pressure.

Once a couple can give each other enjoyable and satisfying experiences through noncoital sex, they are no longer dependent on intercourse as the only source of sexual pleasure. At times when intercourse is not possible for any reason, they can still have sexual enjoyment. If one wants intercourse at a time when the other is not able to respond, a compromise solution is possible. In her function as cook, a wife may on occasion have to express regret that she can't provide her husband with steak; but she can fix him some eggs or some cold chicken—he doesn't have to go hungry. Likewise, in her function as his sex partner, she need not feel, when she is unable to match his desire, that the only alternative is sexual starvation. Noncoital sex can take up the slack and overcome the problem of nonmatching sex patterns.

I repeat, however, that I am not recommending noncoital sex as a way of life for married couples (though in certain unusual situations it can be that). I view it however as a very useful, and in some cases quite essential, step in the process of clearing up some of the stubborn sexual difficulties that many couples encounter. It can clear and prepare the way for the treatment of the sex problem itself. This is true of almost all the recognized sexual inadequacies.

We are now ready to look more closely at these sexual inadequacies, and the best remedies we have so far found in our attempts to resolve them. This will be my purpose in the next chapter.

4.

Understanding

Sexual Inadequacy

The Masters, as I pointed out earlier, have expressed the opinion that something like half of all married couples experience sexual inadequacy of one kind or another. But they have also indicated that, if we were to act promptly and purposefully on the basis of our present knowledge, it should be possible to eliminate sexual inadequacy almost completely in the next ten years. This impressive prospect is largely the result of the very gratifying progress we have made in our understanding of these problems and their treatment, based on the new knowledge which the Masters themselves have assembled for us. I hold these two people, whom I have known personally now for about fifteen years, in the highest esteem; and most of what I have to say in this chapter reflects the findings of their clinical experience, which I have put to good use in my own counseling practice.

So far, in dealing with sexual difficulties in marriage, we have followed a broad avenue along which we could all travel together. Regardless of the precise nature of your problem, the steps I have outlined already should contribute toward resolving it. But now we reach the point at which the broad avenue comes to an end, and a number of signposts point along narrower roads which branch off in different directions. The signposts carry the names we give to the specific forms of sexual inadequacy which married people encounter —three from which husbands may suffer, and three from which wives may suffer. I have already said a little about five of these six specific problems. Now the time has come to go into a little more detail in describing the particular problem and indicating the appropriate treatment. If you want more information than I can provide in this small book, I recommend that you look either at the full report of the Masters,[1] which I must warn you is in highly technical language and not at all easy to read; or at the very readable paperback by Belliveau and Richter,[2] which presents the same material in language more suitable for the lay reader.

Let me begin with sexual inadequacy in the husband, and then proceed to sexual inadequacy in the wife.

Premature Ejaculation

I have already referred to this. The husband goes through the normal sexual cycle. He responds to sexual stimulation, maintains his erection, and goes on to orgasm and ejaculation. The trouble is that he is unable to control the timing, and his orgasm comes too soon. It may come, as in the situation I described in Chapter 2, even before he is able to get his penis into the vagina at all. Or he may be able to get it in, but after only a few movements—and long before his wife has had enough stimulation to bring her to climax—he reaches orgasm and goes limp. He may, however, be able to keep going for quite a while, yet not long enough for a wife who takes a long time to reach the peak of her sexual response. This may, in the case of some wives, be so long that few really stimulated men would be able to hold out.

So a good deal depends on how we interpret the key word "premature." Obviously the man who can't wait even until his erect penis is in the vagina is in trouble. But if he gets it in and is concerned, as men were in the old days, only with his own satisfaction, he may be quite content to ejaculate a minute later—and the wife of

1. William H. Masters and Virginia E. Johnson, *Human Sexual Inadequacy* (Boston: Little, Brown and Company, 1970).
2. Fred Belliveau and Lin Richter, *Understanding Human Sexual Inadequacy* (New York: Bantam Books, Inc., 1970).

the old days might have been quite content for him to get it over and withdraw. In a sense, therefore, premature ejaculation is a condition that has only come to our attention since the husband accepted the task of bringing his wife to orgasm.

This is the most common sexual problem in the husband. In fact, most men probably suffer from it in their early experiences of intercourse, when excitement is great and they have not yet learned control. In time, most of them find ways of delaying their climax, in order to prolong their own pleasure as well as better satisfy their wives. They slow down their responses by lying still for a few moments and then resuming thrusting movements only after their sexual excitement has died down, or they try to switch their minds to something else in the attempt to take their attention off what they are doing. Some try wearing a condom, or even two or three condoms, to reduce sensation. Others use an ointment which will deaden feeling in the penis. Occasionally a man will pinch himself, in the hope that the pain will switch his mind away from sex.

Premature ejaculation, fortunately, is not difficult to cure in most cases. Out of 186 cases treated by the Masters, only 4 were not cured. I have had similar success in treating this problem.

The procedure for husband and wife to follow was first developed by Dr. James Semans, and I happened to be present at the clinical meeting where he first described it, back in the 1950s. The wife stimulates her husband's penis with her hands till he begins to get near to climax. Then he gives her the signal to stop, and they wait till his sexual excitement dies down again. She then repeats the operation. Doing this over and over again enables the man in time to gain control of his sexual desire. Then, with the husband lying on his back and the wife squatting above him, she puts his penis in her vagina and stimulates it with very gentle movements, stopping as before whenever he gives the signal, and repeating the operation when he is ready to begin again. Finally the husband should himself be able to hold back his ejaculation as long as is necessary.

An additional refinement to this training in control was added by the Masters, in the form of what they call the "squeeze technique."

They discovered that the wife could bring about a rapid decrease in her husband's sex desire by pressing the rim below the head of the penis between her fingers and thumb. Details of this are provided in both the books I recommended above. A husband and wife who have already followed my general suggestions in the previous chapter, and then studied the Masters's technique carefully from one of these two books, might be able to carry out these procedures successfully by themselves.

Impotence

This problem, unfortunately, is not so easy to clear up. So if it is your difficulty, it is likely that you will have to seek professional help. But you will give your therapist a much better chance if you and your wife first gain a clear understanding of the problem. And you will be likely to get the best help from a counselor who from the beginning deals with the problem as one involving both you and your wife. I treated one such case in which an impotent husband had for several years been given various kinds of treatment, all without success. His wife had never been brought in; but when he sought my help I asked her to come along to the first interview. It soon became clear that her very subtle performance-demands lay at the root of the trouble, and with her active cooperation the problem was completely cleared up within a few weeks.

We distinguish between *primary* impotence, in which the man has *never* been able to reach orgasm with his penis in the vagina; and *secondary* impotence, in which he *has* been able to perform normal intercourse in times past but has now lost the power to do so. Long-standing primary impotence, in my experience, is very difficult to cure; but fortunately it is not nearly so common as the secondary form.

It should be made clear that on occasion *any* man may suffer from loss of erection and inability to complete sexual intercourse. This can happen as a result of fatigue, shock, drinking too much, or indeed any experience that seriously disturbs sexual arousal. An occasional experience of loss of erection should therefore not be taken very seriously. The danger is that a man may worry so much about such an accident that he will develop enough anxiety to cause it to happen again. Men are very sensitive about loss of erection, because they see this as a serious reflection on their masculinity. Most cultures tend to equate sexual powers in a man with strength and virility.

Another point that should be understood is that impotence *can* be caused by some forms of physical illness; so it is a wise precaution for a man troubled by loss of erection to have a medical checkup before seeking other forms of therapy. The chances are high that there will prove to be no physical cause, but it is a good plan to eliminate this possibility first.

Almost always impotence is caused by anxiety. I have already explained how anxiety "pulls down" sexual desire, and I need not go over this again. Something has happened in the past to give you insecure and negative feelings about having sexual intercourse—for example, early teaching that sex is sinful, or some humiliating experience associated with sex. Sometimes, these early influences can be clearly remembered; in other cases they are long forgotten and buried. But whatever its cause, a threatening shadow falls on the unhappy man just as he is beginning to anticipate an enjoyable sexual experience; a wave of anxiety sweeps over him and his erection ignominiously collapses.

Some men fail in intercourse with a woman because what they really want is another kind of sexual experience, and they are unable to sustain enthusiasm for the experience they are now having. This is true, for example, for the man who has homosexual tendencies, or who has a sexual fetishism. I will say something about these and other sexual "deviations" later in this chapter.

Because of these complex psychological factors, we may ask whether the impotent husband really needs psychotherapy. The Masters are in general skeptical about this, and my experience would confirm their opinion that long-drawn-out treatment of this kind often has disappointing results. All the same, I believe that in the end it may be the only solution for some men, because their sexual failure is really a symptom of personality disorder. My complaint, though, is that psychotherapists often embark on long courses of treatment for impotent men without involving their wives, and without first trying to resolve the problem at a simpler level by behavioral modification. I will speak further of this in the next chapter.

I believe that in almost all cases of impotence a sustained attempt should first be made to clear up the trouble by an extension of the general procedures I have already described. Impotent men don't lack sexual desire. Nearly always they can masturbate. Occasionally a husband who is impotent with his wife can function sexually with another woman. So it is my firm belief that most cases of impotence are caused by a mixture, in varying proportions, of two anxieties: anxiety about sexual intercourse in general, and anxiety about intercourse with the wife in particular. Both of these anxieties should be treated together.

The key question is: What is causing your anxiety about being able to perform sexual intercourse? A complete search must be made for all possible causes. And this should be done by husband and wife together, working on the problem as a team. I believe the best therapist an impotent husband can have is a cooperative wife.

Of course the wife is usually quite taken aback when she is confronted with this idea. But I very often find that, as we discuss the matter, it becomes clear that she does in fact hold the key in her hands. It is I think inevitable that the kindest wife in the world should react with *some* disappointment, and even some resentment, to the fact that her husband can't function sexually. And in less kind wives, this may take the form of thinly veiled disdain and even openly expressed contempt. As long as she sees her husband as a person who *is* a problem to her, rather than as one who *has* a problem which she shares, she humiliates and literally "unmans" him. The first major step in the treatment of impotence, therefore, is to win over the wife, if possible, to the acceptance of a therapeutic role. Unless this can be done, I consider that the chances for his recovery are likely to be poor.

Beyond what I have already said, the process of treatment I have found best is to lead the husband into the anxiety-producing situation by very slow, easy stages. Once the couple can bring each other to orgasm by noncoital sex, I tell them to experiment with putting the penis in the vagina and just lying together in this position. The penis need not be erect, and on no account must they at this stage attempt completed intercourse. The wife must be willing to have her climax later, outside the vagina; she must for the time being allow herself no expectation of anything more than that. The husband may have erections if he wishes, but must avoid any possibility of a climax until after he has withdrawn his penis from the vagina. The object of all this is to reverse the husband's efforts, in the vagina, from trying to reach a climax to trying *not* to do so. A couple should go on with this exercise until they find it quite comfortable and enjoyable—the noncoital climax is always available, so they need not fear frustration. What happens in some cases is that one day the husband, apologetic but smiling, reports that in spite of every effort to restrain himself, he has inadvertently had a climax in the vagina! If this doesn't occur, the couple still have the noncoital sex experiences to support their marriage; and some may accept this as the best they can expect. Others decide to go on to psychotherapy, the prospect for which I believe is made more favorable by what the couple have already achieved.

All this of course assumes a husband and wife who can be patient and fully cooperative. Without these conditions, the basic requirements for finding an acceptable solution of the problem of impotence are not present, and the prospects for the marriage are generally not good.

Ejaculatory Incompetence

This is a condition so rare that I have never encountered it. The Masters, however, found seventeen men—out of all the hundreds they treated—who could sustain erections indefinitely, yet were never able to come to orgasm in the vagina; and they coined the term "ejaculatory incompetence" to describe this condition. The treatment follows very much the same lines as that for impotence. The husband can reach his climiax outside the vagina, and his wife's task is to help him gradually to overcome his resistance to doing so with his penis inside. Of the seventeen men treated by the Masters, all but three were finally able to do this.

Vaginismus

I have already described this distressing problem which some wives experience. It isn't very common, and my impression is that it is becoming less common as women become more comfortable about accepting their sexuality.

The complaint is usually taken to the physician; and this is desirable, because wives may describe what sounds like vaginismus but actually turns out to be something else. So a medical examination, done by a gynecologist if possible, is always desirable. However, be sure that the physician is a kind and understanding person. Otherwise the examination may be so frightening to the wife that it may make her problem worse than before. The Masters recommend that the husband be present at the examination, so that he can see for himself how the wife involuntarily tightens up her muscles and "closes the door."

Why does the wife do this? Because, as a result of negative conditioning in her past, she is scared to death of sex, and particularly of intercourse. Treatment consists of exploring her fears and giving her reassurance. The husband can help to do this, once he clearly understands her problem. When she feels ready, doctor or husband can gently touch her sex organs, or put a finger or two into her vagina, until she can allow this to happen without developing muscular spasm; alternatively, special dilators can be used for this purpose. Once the wife has faced her fears and begun to get rid of her negative ideas and feelings about sex, she should be able to stay relaxed when fingers or dilators are inserted in her vagina, and finally to accept the penis without discomfort. All the women treated by the Masters for vaginismus responded succesfully to this kind of treatment.

Dyspareunia

It could be said that the woman with vaginismus is afraid she is going to be hurt by intercourse. The woman with dyspareunia really *is* hurt; and her pain and distress are just as real if, as happens more often than not, the cause is emotional rather than physical.

Physical causes include lack of sufficient lubrication (I have already discussed this), infections of various kinds which cause burning or itching, malformations, scars left by damage occurring in childbirth or as a result of rape or abortion or following hysterectomy, and cysts and tumors. The possibility of these and other conditions requiring medical attention should be fully explored before coming to the conclusion that the wife is "imagining" the pain.

If it turns out that the trouble is in her mind, this should be treated with sympathy and understanding. We all have a natural protective response to anyone who sticks things in our bodies; and an erect penis is a large object to have pushed deep into your inside. A nervous, apprehensive bride can easily react rather violently to this, even if she knows intellectually that the same thing happens to other women, and that the man who does it has the best of intentions. So long as the sense of apprehension lurks at the back of her mind, she can very easily persuade herself that she is being physically hurt, especially if her husband's movements are vigorous. It is worthwhile to take time to give the wife plenty of understanding, reassurance, and support, until her fears finally vanish and she can welcome intercourse as a pleasant experience.

Orgasm Inadequacy

There is no need for me to describe this condition beyond what I have already done. But I want to go out of my way to discourage the use of the word "frigidity" to refer to it. Even if there is such a thing as a woman as cold as an iceberg, still the word should not be used. Every other term for sexual difficulties in marriage describes the condition as it is experienced by the person who suffers from it. The words "frigidity" passes judgment on the suffering partner. It is obviously a derogatory term invented by males to refer contemptuously to a woman's misfortune. It wouldn't be hard to imagine a corresponding term that women might have seized upon to describe an impotent man—he might for instance, with deadly accuracy, have been called a sexual dropout!

Female orgasm was a rather dark subject until the Masters studied it, and it is still rather puzzling. I know of very little evidence to suggest that female animals or birds have orgasms, though they must have sexual desire and find some enjoyment in the experience. There isn't any real *need* for a woman to have an orgasm, because she doesn't ejaculate as the man does, and she can conceive a child just as well without a climax.

However, the Masters tell us that every woman has the necessary equipment for orgasms, and the natural conclusion is that if she doesn't experience them there's something wrong with her. It is at least reasonable, though, to assume that some women are more orgasmic than others, and this seems to be borne out by clinical evidence; but of course the psychosocial factor may be responsible for this, since we do know that capacity for orgasm depends very much on how free a woman feels inside herself to "let herself go" and enjoy her sexuality.

I am convinced that this is the vital factor that decides whether wives have orgasm or not, and how much they can enjoy the experience. As we have seen, until recently our tradition has frowned on the idea of a woman enjoying sex. Consequently, girls have been brought up to suppress firmly any sexual desires that might stir within them. After years of this it isn't surprising that at marriage, when they try to throw the switch over to the "Release" position, little or nothing happens. Even under the most favorable conditions a woman needs time in order to change her whole attitude toward her sexual feelings from one of restraint to one of encouragement.

If conditions are not favorable, she may fail to effect the change. And if her upbringing was particularly inhibiting with regard to sex, she may be unable to change her attitude even under the most favorable conditions. A few women have been unable to manage it even with the best professional help.

By this time it must be clear that there is a basic reason for sexual inadequacy in the wife, whatever forms the inadequacy may take. The effects vary widely, but the cause is almost always the same. So many influences in her background have conspired to impress upon her that she must protect her sexuality, not only from harm but also from expression, that when favorable conditions occur, she cannot give herself permission to abandon herself to the pleasure that awaits her.

So her need is for help in developing a freer attitude to sexual enjoyment. The treatment follows very similar lines to those I have already described. Once the couple have accepted the idea of non-coital sex, and explored ways in which the husband can arouse his wife to satisfying sexual responses, they may then be encouraged to try penis-vagina experience—but with the wife definitely in control. At first it is best to use the position in which he lies on his back with her squatting above, so that she can experiment playfully with movements which prove to be pleasurable to her. There must be no demand on the part of the husband, and not even the expectation that she will reach a climax. Indeed, it is best for her to be told simply to enjoy the intimacy and actually *avoid* too high levels of sexual excitement, thus reversing the direction of her effort as in the treatment of impotence. By this means she is freed during this period from all performance-demands, either in herself or from her husband—his climax can be brought about in whatever way is agreeable to her.

The treatment of orgasm inadequacy along these lines promises good results. Out of 342 women who brought this problem to the Masters, 4 out of 5 responded satisfactorily to the help they received. In some of those who could not be helped, the trouble lay in an unsatisfactory marriage relationship. It was also found to be decidedly more difficult to help older women to develop orgasm capacity late in life; the failure rate for women of ages 50–79 was twice as high as for all women.

Sexual Deviations

Only a few words can be said on this complicated and controversial subject. Let me begin with a protest against the use of the word "perversion" in this connection; like "frigidity," it is a judgmental term which should be dropped. "Deviation" is a much better term, because it implies not some consciously chosen wickedness but an injury in which the sex drive is turned out of its proper direction —which is actually what has happened. Most sexual deviations are caused by childhood influences, and the damage is done long before the individual is aware of it.

The variety of sexual deviations is quite bewildering, and they are not easy to classify. One way is to divide them into deviations of object and deviations of impulse, though this classification breaks down at some points.

The most common deviation of object is homosexuality, which means that a person of your own sex is more attractive to you than someone of the opposite sex. (The view is being expressed today that homosexuality should be considered not a deviant, but a variant, form of sexuality.) Completely homosexual people, men and women, don't usually marry, but some people are bisexual—they can feel erotic attraction to either sex. Such a person could have difficulty with marital sex relations because he would often prefer a partner of his own sex.

Good examples of deviation of impulse are sadism (sexual excitement produced by acts of cruelty to the partner) and masochism (sexual excitement brought about by being cruelly treated). The sadist is of course a dangerous person; he may do severe damage to his sex partner.

People with sexual deviations do marry, and their partners find their behavior very puzzling. For example, a man with a shoe fetish may be able to develop sexual desire for his wife only if she keeps her shoes on during intercourse.

The treatment of these deviations is usually quite difficult, and should be undertaken only by skilled professional counselors who understand the complex motivations that lie behind them. In general, people with sexual deviations deserve our compassion rather than our condemnation.

On the border line of this subject we find some sexual practices that puzzle many married people. I have already referred to different positions in intercourse and indicated that there is no particular position that is "right." Whatever both partners find acceptable can be done. Similarly, there is really nothing "abnormal" about mouth-genital contacts as a part of sex play. Some couples enjoy such contacts, others find the idea offensive. Even more offensive to most of us is rectal intercourse, though some couples practice it; it may be called unhygienic, but it is difficult to see on what grounds it could be called immoral.

Freedom to try out new ideas is important to married couples, though it could be argued that experiments can be carried too far. On the other hand the prudish rigidity of some couples, which results in a very impoverished sex life, goes too far in the opposite direction. Several rather conservative wives have told me that they had read *The Sensuous Woman*, a best-selling book that describes in detail some of the more unorthodox sexual practices. They reported that, although they could never consider themselves doing some of the things described in the book, on the whole the reading of it had brought home to them how inhibited they had been in their own approaches to sex, and that they had now been able to feel much freer than before to enjoy intercourse with their husbands.

5.

How Professional
Counseling Can Help

In some ways this could be called a do-it-yourself book. I have deliberately tried to explain to you, as simply and clearly as I could, what we now know about sexual-marital difficulties, and the methods of treatment which we are finding to be most effective in dealing with them. I have encouraged you and your marriage partner to try out some of these methods for yourselves, as at least a few steps in the right direction which you could take on your own. In dealing with some of the simpler difficulties, such as premature ejaculation, you could even try out the whole procedure, and you might achieve success together without the need for further help.

However, if I left the matter there, my professional colleagues would accuse me of deceiving you; they would declare that dealing with these problems is in most cases definitely *not* a do-it-yourself operation. And of course they would be right. The truth is that until the Masters offered us greatly improved techniques even the professionals were not doing very well with these problems. I once presented a report of the work of the Masters at an International Medical Congress in Europe, and told the assembled physicians that their overall rate of success, after a five-year follow-up, was about 80 percent. A respected German psychotherapist responded by saying he just didn't believe it! I could understand his incredulity. Most of us have not carried out the kind of follow-up that is part of the Masters's study; but if we had done so, we suspect that our ratio of success would have been a long way under 80 percent.

So, if professional sex counselors, with all their knowledge, skill, and experience, don't always succeed, it is hardly reasonable to suppose that the unaided married couple, merely as a result of reading a small book, can expect miracles to happen. I certainly don't promise you miracles.

All the same, I have written this book because I really believe and hope it will help you. If you have understood and accepted what I have said, you should now see your problem just a little more clearly, and perhaps feel a little less baffled and frustrated about it. You should have caught a glimpse of light at the end of the long, dark tunnel. For there is hardly any sex difficulty in marriage that can't be eased a little by seeing it in clearer perspective. And my hope is that you have gained at least some new insights from the time we have spent together.

The Need for a Competent Therapist

The question is: What is your next step? For at least some readers of this book, it will be to seek out a professional counselor. I want to discuss now what such an approach can offer.

First, the counselor can give you incentive to work at your problem and support in doing so. I have stressed again and again the fact that clearing up marital-sexual difficulties is a joint operation involving husband and wife together. But unless you are recently married or the problem has arisen a short time ago against the background of an otherwise good relationship, you will probably be aware of a crippling paralysis that makes it almost impossible for you both to get anything started together. After a while, couples with sex problems get so discouraged that they seal off the problem area and try to go on living as if it were not there. They don't discuss it any more. They don't even make any further efforts to solve it. They just allow themselves to sink into a state of inertia. Even when one gets a new idea, it seems very difficult to convey it to the other; and if the other doesn't seize upon it eagerly, nothing further is done. So there is a chronic lack of motivation to open up the question again, because by this time it has become a sensitive and painful area of the relationship.

Seeking counseling helps break through this inertia. Even if only one partner makes the first move, the other is likely to respond when the counselor—as he always should—invites his or her cooperation. Now the problem is being tackled by a team of three, and the counselor can keep things moving even if the couple becomes temporarily deadlocked, as often happens. This facilitating role of the counselor, quite apart from his specialized knowledge, is of great importance to the couple, because it commits them to take action.

But a good counselor does much more than this. He sees the whole situation from the outside, and can therefore put his finger on the critical areas which the couple themselves may not be aware of. He also enables them to communicate with each other, and to overcome any embarrassment they have had in speaking about their sexual feelings and responses. He further helps them to bring out into the open negative and hostile feelings which they couldn't express to one another except for his presence, because alone they would simply end up hurting each other and fighting each other. The counselor provides a safe, protected arena where all kinds of hurt and angry feelings can be expressed, interpreted, and discharged. And he can then encourage the reawakening of warm and tender feelings that have been frozen and buried out of sight, but which can spring up and blossom again in a warmer climate.

Above all, the counselor can provide the couple with a trustworthy person in whom both can place their confidence, and who can guide them along the sometimes rough and rocky road they must travel to find the solution to their problem. He can help them to agree on a sound plan of treatment that they can carry out together under his supervision and with his support.

What Action You Should Take

What kind of commitment would this involve for you? It would mean, of course, a series of counseling interviews—with each of you separately and with both together. Few sex problems can be cleared up in one interview, and some take a long time. You would have to be willing to give the counselor a reasonable chance by working with him over weeks and months. You can't expect a problem that has developed over many years to be reversed easily or quickly—that is simply unreasonable. And professional counseling usually costs money, because the people who do it are highly qualified specialists. But you pay out money for many other things that are of much less value and importance than your happiness together as husband and wife, so this expenditure should be seen in that perspective.

You should understand that counselors work in a variety of ways. I have already discussed the long-term analytical approach of the pychotherapist, which I personally do not consider to be the most promising way of dealing with marital-sexual troubles. The Masters also rejected this approach in favor of what is called behavior modification—a direct attempt to get people, under professional supervision, to experiment with new and different ways of relating to each other, in contrast with the method of getting them to change their way of thinking and feeling about themselves, and leaving them to work out the appropriate new courses of action. Most experienced marriage and sex counselors, however, including the Masters, use a combination of both of these approaches, but with much less emphasis on digging into the past than in the practice of psychotherapy.

Almost all marriage counselors treat husband and wife together, with the emphasis on their relationship. The Masters took over this approach, but carried it even further. They worked as a team of co-therapists, so that a man and a woman together served as counselors to husband and wife together. This concept is basic to the Masters's philosophy; and there are some strong arguments in its favor. But at the present time very few co-therapist teams have been trained and are in action, so you probably wouldn't be able to get this kind of treatment. It is my own view that most of the basic principles of the Masters's method *can* be used by a single counselor, though this may be something short of the ideal.

How do you find a competent and trustworthy counselor? That's a highly important question, and I want to give you a reliable answer.

I have to tell you that some caution is necessary. Marriage and sex counseling is a new field, and it is not as strictly controlled yet as, for example, the long-established fields of medicine and law. So there are some people around who call themselves marriage counselors, but are poorly qualified. There are even a few who are outright quacks.

It is best to find someone who can be confidently recommended by a professional person you already know and trust—your physician or pastor, for example. If you can't do this, don't trust the yellow pages of the telephone directory, to which you turn for plumbers and electricians; it is in these pages that the quacks advertise themselves, along with the competent counselors, and you must have some way of distinguishing one from the other. A good plan is to seek guidance from your nearest Family Service Agency, or a mental health clinic, or the psychology department of your local college or university. If there are members of the American Association of Marriage and Family Counselors in your community, you can rely on them, because they have to measure up to high standards in order to be accepted. If you enclose a stamped self-addressed return envelope, the national headquarters of the AAMFC at 6211 W. Northwest Highway, Dallas, Texas 75225, will give you names of members in your locality.

Even when you find a counselor, you may want to check out his qualifications. No competent professional person will mind being asked questions about his credentials—in fact, he will welcome it. Before making an appointment you can ask him or his secretary how he works, and what his fees are. He should accept you for treatment as a married couple; experience now proves this to be the most effective approach. And he should be willing to make an evaluation of your situation after the first few interviews, so that you can consider the prospects and decide whether you want to face the expense of continued visits. If after working with him long enough to arrive at a fair judgment, you and your partner are not satisfied with his treatment, you can discontinue and try again with another counselor. It is of great importance that you should have complete confidence in what your counselor is doing, and you may not find one who suits you at the first try. All professional people understand this.

Professional Qualifications and Competence

Who *are* the professional people best qualified to deal with sex problems? That's a very difficult question to answer, but I will try.

Most people naturally think of the physician first. The fact must be faced, however, that in the medical school curriculum there has been little or nothing about sexual inadequacy, and what the medical student learns he has to pick up where he can. This is being changed quite rapidly today, and tomorrow's doctor will be better equipped. But the average senior physician of today has neither the training, the time, nor the inclination to get involved in dealing with sexual inadequacy in any depth. There are some conspicuous exceptions to this general rule, however, and when a doctor is also a well-qualified marriage and sex counselor, there is no better source of aid.

What about psychiatrists? Some of them are highly skilled in this field. Others, unfortunately, are not. The psychotherapist, as we have seen, is generally committed to the traditional methods of psychoanalysis, which insist that the therapist treat only one patient in an extended series of interviews. People committed to this view are very unwilling, naturally, to work with husband and wife together, which is a serious disadvantage. For clearing up deep-seated personality problems in the individual, psychotherapy is in my opinion the best treatment available. But it has not been conspicuously successful in dealing with sexual and marital problems. Many younger psychiatrists, and some older ones, are today aware of this, and are using the new approaches. Check this with the individual psychiatrist you have in mind.

Psychologists? Only a small proportion of them are trained in the clinical field, and many of those are still committed, as the psychiatrists are, to the traditional methods. So investigate quite carefully the training and approach of any psychologist you have in mind as a counselor.

Social workers? Some of them, who have had special training in the field, are superb marriage counselors. Their training, unlike that of the other helping professions, is much more practical than theoretical, and their system of supervision tends to make them very capable clinicians. But many social workers have specialized in other areas, and have no special competence in this field.

Pastors, priests, and rabbis? To an increasing extent the seminaries are providing good training in counseling today, and the standard of competence among the younger members of this profession is rising rapidly. Some of the really good pastoral counselors (especially if they are clinical members of the American Association of Pastoral Counselors) are very good indeed. On the other hand, nearly every pastor considers himself to be a counselor, and some of them are so poorly qualified both personally and professionally that they should never attempt to deal with sexual or marital problems; but they do, and sometimes the results are disastrous. So again, walk warily here; but if you find a competent man, he will probably be very helpful to you.

Besides these, there are occasionally people belonging to other professions—lawyers, nurses, sociologists, and teachers—who have taken the time to inform themselves, and to seek training in the fields of sex and marriage counseling. The situation can be summed up by saying that there is no particular profession, *all* of whose members are qualified in this field; and there is probably no profession that has not produced a few really good counselors.

Conclusion

Sexual difficulties in marriage are distressing. They often mean shattered dreams and disappointed hopes. They may create resentment and hostility that can slowly poison a marriage. Our record of dealing with them in the past has been pretty dismal. The sad truth is that we were so ignorant that we were largely blundering in the dark. Our culture cast a heavy shadow over sex. It was under a taboo, and people were given little encouragement either to investigate it or to enjoy it.

All that is now changing, quite rapidly, and it is no longer necessary for people who have marital-sexual problems to suffer silently. Patience, as Clement of Alexandria once put it, is "the knowledge of what is to be endured and what is not." There are burdens in life that we have to carry with all the fortitude we can muster: incurable illness, financial disasters, bereavement, ambitions that cannot be fulfilled. But there are other human situations that need no longer be endured, because the burden can now be lifted from our shoulders.

Sexual inadequacy is one of these. A flood of new knowledge has begun to reach us. We see much more clearly than we did. We are learning new skills. We are getting far better results than ever before. There are still some burdens we seem unable to lift—even the Masters, with all their resources, failed to help about one-fifth of those who were sent to them. But for each of these unfortunates, four *were* helped. That means hope for millions.

So skilled help is available. Not so much of it as we could wish, yet. But more and more people are learning, receiving training, and taking their places in the ranks of the helpers. These resources are available, and available to you. Make use of them. It is your privilege and your right.